Higher and Higher

Written by Liz Miles

Collins

Chains keep this chair high.

3

Jack checks a pair of lights.

4

Dee shoots foam.

7

Asher uncurls sails on a ship.

Mark feels no fear.

Wings keep Gail up.

12

13

How high?

After reading

Letters and Sounds: Phase 3

Word count: 58

Focus phonemes: /ai/ /ee/ /igh/ /oa/ /oo/ /oo/ /ar/ /ur/ /ow/ /ear/ /air/ /er/

Common exception words: the, go, no, I, of

Curriculum links: Understanding the World: The World

Early learning goals: Reading: use phonic knowledge to decode regular words and read them aloud accurately; demonstrate understanding when talking with others about what they have read

Developing fluency

- Your child may enjoy hearing you read the book. Model fluency and expression.
- Practise reading out the speech bubbles with your child using expression.
- Encourage your child to sound talk and then blend the words, e.g. /u/n/c/ur/l/s **uncurls**. It may help to point to each sound as your child reads.
- Then ask your child to reread the sentence to support fluency and understanding.

Phonic practice

- Look through the book. What words can your child find with the /ai/ sound? (*chains, chair, pair, sails, Gail*)
- Can they think of any words that rhyme with the word **near**? These words have the /ear/ sound at the end. (e.g. *fear, tear, hear, dear, gear*)

Extending vocabulary

- Ask your child:
  - The book is about going **higher**. What is the opposite of higher? (*lower*)
  - On page 10 Mark feels **no fear**. What other words mean fear? (e.g. *dread, fright, worry*)
  - What is the opposite of "fearful"? How could you describe Mark? (e.g. *brave, courageous, fearless, talented*)